HEALTHIER CHOICES
HEALTHIER BODIES

HEALTHIER CHOICES HEALTHIER BODIES

A lower fat, and lower sugar

Peggy Kleiter

To order additional copies of this book, contact:
Xlibris Corporation
1-888-795-4274
www.Xlibris.com
Orders@Xlibris.com
125174

CONTENTS

WRITING THIS BOOK has given me a lot of enjoyment. It has let me do one of the things I love the most and that is to cook for people to enjoy. We all think that food should be full of fat and sugar to taste good, that is so not true, if we just stand back and look at the fat free products that are available to us on our grocery shelves.

I do use sugar substitutes and some natural sugars, as we all seem to love sweetness and can't get away from that and I am no different. There comes a time when we all have to stand back and look at ourselves, we can either like what we see or not, the only one who can do anything about their weight is themselves. I definitely did not like what I seen at 300 pounds. I felt lousy and had a hard time getting around. I got to be 300 pounds by eating good food made by old fashion cooks as 50 years ago food and cooking options were limited either by availability or technology.

Well I know how to cook and I am good at it, but I guess I needed to teach myself how easy it is to make a lot of great tasting food that everyone could enjoy and not feel like your gaining weight or on a diet. Diets don't work anyway; you need to lead a healthy lifestyle.

To have a healthy body I am not saying you can eat has much has you want, but you can still have an extra serving and not feel guilty or have dessert if you make it yourself, because it's difficult to find good low fat "and" low sugar meals, but you can buy the ingredients to make them, and I will share with you a few of my favorites.

But before I do i would like everyone to think about how easy it is to spend a lot of money eating out, which usually are high fat and high sugar foods, so we have to put a little more effort and thought into what we feed our bodies. Good nutrition goes a long way to making us feel better. Proper portions and good easy food make it all worthwhile, but with a little bit of work to feel good there is nothing more worth it. With good food and exercise there is no reason why we shouldn't feel great at any age.

I know that I feel better being fit at 40+ then I did when I was 14 and overweight! Many of the people I know asked me how I did it lose all that weight. I tell them I started by changing the way I cook. My girlfriend gave me a low fat cookbook so that's were i started, but it was not enough for me to lose weight. So i decided to start eliminating sugars and writing recipes down have I changed them so i could go back and make them again. I have had many people ask me where the recipe from is. I always say probably from a couple a different recipes with my own twist thrown in to try and keep food tasting good. Well I have had enough people ask me for my recipes, so I decided I would like to share them with the world.

We are an overweight society because we have been taught to cook with lots of fat and sugar. I promise you, you might taste a difference with some food, but it's because you taste the flavor of the grains. I do like to stay with more natural grains that are not bleached and majorly processed.

I love to feed my cookies and muffins to kids to ask them what they think. Surprisingly enough I have not had a lot of kids say anything other than "it's good, can I have another one." Maybe our children would eat better, if when we are offering them snacks and meals we offer healthier choices. So on your next shopping trip for groceries pick up a bag of splenda, some whole wheat flour, and have a look at the actual nutritional value to food. Try and keep some whole wheat noodles or if you must have white buy the Catelli smart on hand instead of whites. Try and buy has low of milk fats has possible you can buy lots of low fat and fat free dairy products.

Quinoa is an ancient grain that is a good grain but most of us don't know how to cook it, it can be a great side dish. I hope you enjoy them has much has I do they are a great replacement for rice. There are many foods we can eat that aren't has harmful to our bodies, we just have to choose them when you're in the sugar isle try to buy natural raw brown sugar and not the processed white.

Honey is another great sweetener and its natural, but careful brown sugar and honey are still sugar and that adds up to calories and fat. You should probably browse the recipes see what you would like to try and if you don't have the ingredients put them on your shopping list

(While you're there park at the far end at the parking lot, it's a great way to get a little extra exercise!)

I hope this inspires everyone who tries these recipes to maintain a healthier lifestyle and enjoy their meal and be able to eat their cake to. As I said, I love to cook, so I am always writing new recipes. There will be some that you won't get to try because I'll have completed them after I am done writing this book. I hope you all enjoy these recipes enough to try and make your own, or to look forward to more recipes I may have to publish at a later date.

Well i think it's time to get down to business and share those recipe's with you and teach you some tricks on making your own sugar free pie filling and oat flour you'll be surprised how easy it is! I am going to give you some ideas for all the meals of the day and even host a dinner party that won't make anyone feel quality about the meal and the dessert.

BUNS AND BREADS

Quick 60% Whole Wheat Buns

3 cups warm/hot water

3 tbsp. quick rise yeast

¼ cup canola oil

5 cups whole wheat flour

2/3 cups splenda

¼ cup egg white

1 tsp. salt

3 cups white flour

Place water in a large bowl. Add splenda, salt, eggs and oil mixing together. In a separate bowl combine flours and yeast together mixing well. Gradually add the flour to the water mixture to make a soft but not sticky dough. Let rise 15 minutes, punch down dough. Repeat 2 more times. Make dough into buns let rise 1 hour. Bake for 15-20 minutes at 350 or until tops are golden. To ensure all your dough recipes rise properly. Place bowl on a towel, and cover with another towel. Always keep your doughs covered while rising, and away from any drafts.

Pineapple Bread

2 cups whole wheat flour

2 tbsp. baking powder

1 tsp. salt

½ cup splenda

1 tsp. baking soda

1 can crushed pineapple in own juice (no extra 1 cup packed grated zucchini sugar added)

¼ cup skim or 1% milk

1 tsp. vanilla extract

Add all dry ingredients. Mix to blend slightly. Add pineapple and juice mix. Add remaining ingredients, mixing by hand well. Bake in bread pan at 350°F for 40-45 minutes.

Pumpkin Bread

2 cups whole wheat flour

2 tsp. baking soda

1 tsp. cinnamon

1 tsp. salt

½ cup splenda

¾ cup orange juice

2 tsp. baking powder

½ tsp. nutmeg

½ tsp. ginger

1 ½ cups mashed pumpkin

1 tsp. vanilla

½ cup pecans or nut of choice (optional)

Combine all dry ingredients in bowl, set aside and mix all wet ingredients thoroughly. Gradually add dry ingredients mixing by hand just until moistened. Place in bread pan and bake for about 1 hour or until toothpick comes out clean at 350°F.

Almond Craisin Bread

3 cups whole wheat flour

1 ½ tsp. baking powder

1 ¾ cup buttermilk

2 tsp. vanilla extract

1 cup slivered almonds

½ cup splenda

1 tsp. baking soda

2 tbsp. honey

1 cup craisins

Combine all dry ingredients in bowl. Add buttermilk, honey and vanilla and mix well by hand. Add craisins and almonds. Place in bread pan and bake for approximately 40-50 minutes on 350°F.

Whole Wheat Sweet Dough

To make buttermilk add 1 tbsp. Vinegar to 1 cup low fat milk if you don't happen to keep milk in your home, try to keep nonfat milk powder on hand, then you can always make milk.

¼ cup warm water	2 tbsp. quick rise yeast
1/3 cup splenda	3/4 cup white flour
11/4 cup whole wheat flour	¾ cup oat flour
½ tsp. salt	½ cup buttermilk (room temperature)

Place water, yeast and 1 tbsp. splenda in a bowl, set aside. Place remaining sugar and dry ingredients together in a bowl, mix well. Add yeast mixture and buttermilk to dry ingredients gradually making sure you can form soft dough. Coat tough with cooking spray, set aside, let rise for 1 hour or until doubled in size making sure to cover dough so it stay's warm. This is also great for cheese loafs, cinnamon buns, and more.

To make buttermilk add 1 tbsp. Vinegar to 1 cup low fat milk if you don't happen to keep milk in your home, try to keep nonfat milk powder on hand, then you can always make milk.

Whole Wheat Bread

11/2 cups warm water   2 tsp. traditional yeast

1 tbsp. splenda

In a large bowl combine above ingredients and let rise about 10 minutes or until foamy

2 tsp. quick rise yeast   1 tsp. salt

1 1/2 tsp. skim milk powder   1 tbsp. lard

2 cups whole wheat flour   1 cup multigrain flour

Combine all the above dry ingredients including the yeast before adding to the wet yeast mixture. Once wet yeast mixture is done rising add the dry flour yeast mixture to the wet, before kneading add the lard mix well. Knead dough for at least 10 minutes let rise 30 minutes, knead dough again for another 10 minutes let rise another 30 minutes, knead dough again for another 10 minutes when done kneading place dough in loaf pan let rise for 1 hour. Make sure you cover your dough when letting rise to keep it warm, and does not get any type of draft, has this will affect how the dough will rise. After bread has risen for 1 hour make sure your oven is preheated to 350 bake for 50 minutes.

SOUPS

Lentil Soup

1 carton chicken broth

1 ½ cup lentils

3 celery stalks chopped

1 tsp. ground cumin

1 tsp. salt

2 cups grated cabbage

2 chopped tomatoes

1 red onion chopped

1 tbsp. minced garlic

1 tsp. pepper

Combine all ingredients in medium size pot. Cook over medium heat for at least 1 hour.

Mushroom Soup

*This is not low fat but if you wish it to be use 1% milk and 1/2 package fat free cream cheese instead of the heavy whipping cream, you will still need 1 cup heavy cream, or this will not be very creamy.

1 lb. fresh mushrooms

1 litre heavy whipping cream

3 celery stalks chopped

4 tbsp. dill weed

1 tsp. seasoning salt

1 tbsp. minced garlic

1 carton vegetable broth

1 onion chopped

½ cup water

1 tsp. salt and pepper

1 tsp. oregano spice

Slice mushrooms; add onions and celery brown in a non-stick frying pan until all are tender. In a dutch oven pot combine broth and mushroom mixture with all the mushroom juice and spices, simmer on medium heat for 1 hour. After simmered, add cream. Cook for approximately 20 minutes. Mix water and cornstarch to make a paste. Add to soup gradually until thickened to your taste. Serve and enjoy.

Vegetable Soup

½ cup frozen peas

¼ cup corn

2 tomatoes

4 medium carrots

3 bok choy stalks

2 small potatoes

1 large can crushed tomatoes

½ cup beans

1 onion

3 celery stalks

1 medium red pepper

¼ cup sliced mushrooms

1 carton vegetable broth

Seasoning salt/dill weed/salt/pepper/oregano/garlic (optional)

Chop all vegetables into bite size and add to broth and crushed tomatoes. Add selected seasons to your taste. Simmer on medium heat until all vegetables are tender.

Beef Barley Soup

1 lb. chopped beef

1 cup barley

3 medium potatoes

3 celery stalks

2 cloves garlic

4 tbsp. beef soup base

8 cups water (approximately)

1 onion

3 large carrots

2 tomatoes

1 can crushed tomatoes

Seasoning salt/dill weed/salt/pepper (optional)

Place beef in pot to brown. Once beef is browned, add water and simmer on low heat for at least 3 hours. After 3 hours, add remaining ingredients. Add selected seasons to your taste. Simmer until all are soft and cooked. Should be about 2 hours.

Chicken Noodle Soup

Roasted chicken carcass or 3 chicken legs backs attached

8 cups water

2 onions

1 celery bunch

4 carrots chopped very small

2 cloves garlic

Seasoning salt/dill weed/salt/ pepper (optional)

2 cups noodle of choice

Remove skin from chicken and place in water with all spices. Simmer on medium/low heat for 2 hours. Add celery, garlic, onions, carrots and noodles. Add selected seasons to your taste. Simmer for 1 hour.

Bean Soup

1 left over ham bone

1 lb. well cooked bacon

8-12 cups water

2 cups yellow beans

2 cups yellow split peas

1 onion chopped

3 celery stalks chopped

2 cloves garlic minced

2 medium potatoes chopped

Seasoning salt/dill weed/salt/pepper (optional)

½ cup barley (optional)

Boil ham bone and bacon for 30 minutes in water, and then simmer for approximately 4 hours. Strain the ham bone and bacon in strainer to remove any bones/cartilage. Place all meat and juice back in pot and add remaining ingredients. Add selected seasons to your taste. Simmer on low heat approximately 1 hour or until all is tender. To make thicker, use the cornstarch paste from mushroom soup recipe.

Whole Wheat Seafood Wraps

4 whole wheat soft tortilla shells	1 package fat free cream cheese
½ cup fat free sour cream	3 tbsp. fat free miracle whip
1 tbsp. dill weed/salt/pepper/ seasoning salt	1 can shrimp
1 can crab	½ cup grated mozzarella
½ cup seafood sauce	any type of large leaf green

Combine cream cheese, sour cream, miracle whip, seafood sauce and spices. Beat until smooth, and then mix in by hand shrimp, crab and grated cheese. Let mixture stand in refrigerator for at least 1 hour covered. Place tortilla shell on flat surface, cover edge of shell with green then spread mixture over entire shell. Roll and cut into bite size pieces.

Wheat Pizza Rolls

Use Quick 60% Whole Wheat Buns (pg 11) recipe for dough

500 g salami	500 g pepperoni
1 onion	1 pepper (red is best)
1 jar spaghetti sauce	2 cups grated mozzarella

Fry meat, onions and peppers, set aside and let cool. Mix in cheese and sauce. Roll out dough on floured surface to about ¼ inch thickness. Spread meat mixture over entire surface. Roll dough into a tube. Cut into about 2 inch rolls. Place on parchment paper in 9x13 pans. Let rise covered with a towel for 1 hour (They can rise for up to 2 hours without hurting them). Bake for 15-20 minutes at 350°F.

You could also cut your dough into rectangles or circles. Placing spoonfuls of mixture into the center of dough pieces pinch shut on all sides. Let rise like you would rolls. Kids love these they think their pizza pops.

On The Run Dog

Use Quick 60% Whole Wheat Buns (pg 11) recipe for dough

1-2 dozen hot dogs/smokies of your choice
2 cups grated cheese of your choice
1 jar of salsa

   Roll out dough to about 8 inch wide and ½ inch thick. Cut strips wide enough for hot dog (3 inches). Place a hot dog on dough. Spread about 1 tsp. of salsa along hot dog and top with cheese. Then roll each one and pinch all ends shut. Place on parchment paper in 9x13 baking dishes. Cover with towel and let rise for 1 hour. Bake for 15-20 minutes on 350°F. Remove and place on cooling racks. For easy freezing, place in Ziploc bags. Microwave for 90 seconds.

Eggs on the go

Use quick 60 percent whole wheat dough recipe from page 11.

1 dozen eggs
1 cup cubed ham
1/4 cup sliced mushrooms
1 small onion chopped
1/2 cup grated low fat cheese your choice

1 pkg bacon
1/4 cup chopped orange pepper
1/4 cup chopped tomatoes
1/2 cup salsa

   In a large frying pan scramble eggs, when just about cooked add cooked bacon and the remaining ingredients finish cooking. Once cooked set aside to cool. When dough is ready to use roll out dough to about 1/2 inch thickness, and cut into rectangles. Place a large tablespoon of egg mixture into dough pocket and pinch dough closed on all sides. Place on a cookie sheet a let rise again for 1 hour. Bake on 350 for 20-25 minutes. You should never skip breakfast, its the meal that gets our bodies going for the day. These freeze great just take one out warm it in the microwave and breakfast is served. ENJOY!

Low Fat Spinach Dip

1 250 g package cream cheese fatfree	1 cup fat free sour cream
1 package Knorrs vegetable soup mix	1 small onion finely chopped
1 package thawed chopped spinach	1 tbsp. dill weed
1 tbsp. seasoning salt	1 tsp. salt
1 tsp. pepper	1 tbsp. minced garlic

Combine all ingredients. Place in smaller dipping bowls. Serve with cut up Quick 60% Whole Wheat Buns.

Corn Relish

12 large cobs	3 large onions diced
8 celery stalk finely chopped	1 large green pepper
2 large red peppers	3 medium size zucchini
5 tbsp. pickling salt	4 tbsp. dry mustard
6 tbsp. turmeric	4 cups vinegar
4 cups brown sugar	1 cup sugar
½ cup water	6 tbsp. cornstarch

Combine first 12 ingredients in large pot, bring to a boil. Continue cooking for 2 hours stirring frequently in the last 30 minutes. In a cup, combine water and cornstarch, mix until smooth, and add to relish to thicken once done cooking. Place jars in canner for at least 25 minutes on a rolling boil.

Make sure corn is cut off cob and cleaned thoroughly. Chop all remaining vegetables very finely.

DESSERTS

Low Sugar Fudge

1 package semi-sweet chocolate (8 bars)

1 ½ cup sweetened condensed milk

¼ cup butter

¼ cup splenda

½ cup slivered almonds

1 tsp. vanilla

Combine all ingredients in pot over low-medium heat stirring frequently. Cook for about 10-15 minutes keeping batter smooth. Remove from head. Add vanilla and almonds. Stir in until smooth. Place in 8x8 pan lined with parchment paper. Cool in fridge 8 hours or until firm.

Healthier Cinnamon Rolls

2 cups whole wheat flour	1 cup white flour
1 cup oat flour	½ cup oat bran
1 ½ cups medium hot water	3 tbsp. quick rise yeast
1 ¼ cup splenda	3 tbsp. canola oil
½ tsp. salt	1 egg
1 cup margarine	3 tbsp. brown sugar
2 cups raisins optional	Cinnamon

Place water in a large bowl. Adding the eggs and oil mix together. In a separate bowl combine flours, yeast, salt and splenda mixing dry together. Gradually add the flour mixture to the wet to make a soft but not sticky dough. Let rise for 30 min punch down let rise an additional 30 minutes after this roll dough into a large rectangle approximately 1/2 inch thick. Using low fat margarine or 50/50 blend, soften to spread roughly 1/8 inch thickness. Over rolled dough sprinkle approximately 1 cup splenda make sure your dough is well covered with the splenda. Sprinkle approximately 3 TBSP brown sugar on top of the sugar sprinkle entire dough generously with cinnamon. Finally top with raisins. Starting at one end roll dough. Once rolled completely cut into about 3 inch pieces. Place rolls on parchment paper in 9 x13 pans let rise an additional hour then bake at 350 for 20 to 25 minutes. If you don't want to use margarine you can use butter, the rolls will just be a little higher in fat ENJOY!

Chocolate-Chocolate Wheat Chip Cookies

1 cup whole wheat flour

¼ cup non-fat milk powder

3 tbsp. brown sugar

¼ cup prune pureed or butternut squash

3 tbsp. sugar free cocoa

½ cup splenda

¾ tsp. baking soda

1 tsp vanilla extract

Add flour, cocoa, milk powder and sugar together in a bowl. Mix well to ensure no lumps of flour etc. Add baking soda to dry ingredients and mix well. Stir in prune pureed and vanilla stirring until moistened. If does not add ¼ tsp. water at a time until moist. Stir in chips. Drop spoonful onto parchment paper lined cookie sheets. Bake at 350°F for about 9 minutes.

Peanut Butter Banana Cookies

1 large or 2 medium banana

½ cup splenda

½ cup white flour

¼ cup egg whites (from carton)

½ tsp. baking powder

½ tsp. cinnamon

1 tsp. vanilla

¾ cup peanut butter

3 tbsp. pure cane brown sugar

½ cup whole wheat flour

½ tsp. baking soda

1 tsp. salt

1 cup sugar free chocolate chips

Combine and beat banana, peanut butter and sugars until smooth. Mix in egg white and vanilla, then add remaining ingredients except chocolate chips and mix well. Stir in chocolate chips. Roll into about 1 inch balls and flatten with fork. Bake at 350°F for 9-11 minutes.

Apple Oat Muffins

3 apples chopped into small chunks

1 cup oats

¼ cup oat flour

½ cup whole wheat flour

½ cup white flour

¼ cup oat bran

1 tsp. vanilla extract

1 cup fat free vanilla yogurt

2 heaping tbsp. baking powder

1 tsp. baking soda

½ cup splenda

½ cup liquid egg white

1 tsp. cinnamon

¼ cup apple sauce

1 tsp. salt

¼ tsp. nutmeg

Mix apple sauce, yogurt, egg white and vanilla, add dry ingredients. Mix well. Add chopped apples. If too dry or stiff while mixing, add extra yogurt or apple sauce. Place in muffin pans. Bake at 350°F for approximately 20-25 minutes or until tooth pick comes out clean.

Topping For Apple Oat Muffins

¾ cup oats

3 tbsp. whole wheat flour

3 tbsp. low fat margarine

½ cup splenda

3 tbsp. brown sugar

Mix until crumbly. Place on top of muffins before baking.

Raisin Wheat Bran Muffin

¾ cup vanilla fat free yogurt or fat free sour cream

¾ cup apple sauce

¼ cup liquid egg white

½ cup oat bran

1 cup all bran

1 cup whole wheat flour

1 ½ cups boiled raisins (drained)

1 tsp. vanilla

1 tsp. cinnamon

1 tsp. salt

2 tbsp. baking powder

1 tsp. baking soda

½ cup splenda

Mix yogurt, sauce, egg white, splenda, oat bran and all bran. Set aside. Cook raisins for at least 5 minutes over medium-high heat. Drain leaving a little water with raisins. Combine remaining ingredients to yogurt mixture. Stir in raisins. Spray muffin pans well or use paper liners. Bake at 350°F for 20-25 minutes or until toothpick comes out clean.

Blueberry Wheat Muffins

¾ cup 0% fat blueberry yogurt

1 cup sugar free Motts blueberry/ apple sauce

¼ cup egg whites

½ cup splenda

½ cup frozen blueberries

¼ cup oat flour

1 cup whole wheat flour

¼ cup oat bran

1 tsp. vanilla extract

1 tsp. salt

2 tbsp. baking powder

1 tsp. baking soda

Mix all wet ingredients except berries. Mix in dry ingredients and lightly stir in berries. Spray muffin tins or use paper liners. Bake at 350°F for 20-25 minutes or until toothpick comes out clean.

Low Fat Carrot Cake

½ cup whole wheat flour

½ cup oat flour

1 cup white flour

2 tsp. baking powder

½ tsp. baking soda

1 cup raisins (optional)

1 tsp. salt

1 ½ cup splenda

1/2 cup canola oil

1 cup liquid egg white

2 cups grated carrots

Combine whole wheat flour, oat flour, white flour, baking soda, baking powder, splenda and salt. Then mix in canola oil, egg whites and grated carrots. Stir in raisins. Place in 13x13 greased pan. Bake at 350°F for 40-60 minutes, checking regularly after 40 minutes. For icing see page.

White Caramel Topped Cake

¼ cup whole wheat flour

¼ cup oat flour

¾ cup splenda

¾ tsp. baking powder

½ cup caramel syrup

¼ cup white flour

¼ cup cocoa

¾ tsp. baking soda

1 tsp. salt

2/3 cup fat free sour cream

Sift flours, baking powder, baking soda and salt into a medium size bowl. Beat in remaining ingredients. Pour into well-greased 9 inch spring form pan. Bake at 350°F for 30-35 minutes. While still hot, drizzle heavily with caramel syrup.

Chocolate Raspberry Crumb Cake

¼ cup whole wheat flour

¼ cup oat flour

¾ cup splenda

¾ tsp. baking powder

3 cups frozen raspberries thawed

1 tsp. vanilla extract

¼ cup white flour

¼ cup cocoa

¾ tsp. baking soda

1 tsp. salt

½ cup plain fat free yogurt

Place and mix well flours and all dry ingredients in medium size bowl. Add raspberries, juice, and all wet ingredients. Stir to mix well. Place in a well-greased 9 inch spring form pan.

Topping

½ cup walnuts

3 tbsp. brown sugar

2 tbsp. sugar free chocolate syrup

2 tbsp. whole wheat flour

¼ cup splenda

Combine all ingredients until crumbly. Sprinkle over base. Drizzle approximately 2 tbsp. chocolate syrup lightly. Bake at 350°F for about 35 minutes. The top should spring back up when lightly touched.

Quick Cheesecake

1 ½ cup graham crumbs

1 tub sugar free cool whip

3 tbsp. fat & sugar free lemon pudding mix

3 tbsp. melted margarine

1 package fat free cream cheese

Pie filling/fresh fruit of choice

Mix graham crumbs and margarine in a bowl. Press into 8x8 pan. Bake at 350°F for 8 minutes. Cool. Combine cream cheese, cool whip and pudding mix in bowl, blending until smooth. Top with pie filling/ toppings. Refrigerate for at least 3 hours if serving with fresh fruit top before serving.

Blueberry Cheesecake

2 cups graham crumbs

2 tbsp. low far margarine

3 tbsp. splenda

Filling

2 cups sugar free sweetened condensed milk

1 tsp. lemon juice

¾ cup egg whites

2 blocks fat free cream cheese

2 tsp. vanilla extract

¾ cup splenda

¾ cup pie filling

Combine first 3 ingredients and press into lightly grease 9 inch spring form pan. For filling combine all ingredients except pie filling. Blend well until smooth. Pour over base. Drop spoonfuls of pie filling into filling and use a knife to swirl into filling.

PEGGY KLEITER

Chocolate Swirly Cheesecake

2 cups graham crackers   3 tbsp. splenda
2 tbsp. low fat margarine

Combine and press into lightly greased 9 inch spring form pan.

Filling

2 blocks fat free cream cheese   2 cups sugar free condensed milk
2 tsp. vanilla extract   ½ cup egg white (carton)
½ cup splenda

Mix all ingredients until smooth. Pour over base. (Set aside approximately ½ cup)

Chocolate Swirl

2 tbsp. cocoa   ¼ cup splenda
½ tsp. vanilla extract   2 tbsp. sugar free chocolate syrup

Mix well into the ½ cup cheese mixture. Pour in swirls over other filling. Using a knife, run it through for deeper swirls.

Pistachio Pudding Dessert

1 package fat & sugar free
pistachio pudding mix
1 ½ cup melted margarine

1 tub sugar free cool whip
1 can crushed pineapple in own juice
1 ½ cup graham crumbs

Melt margarine in a bowl and add crumbs. Mix and press into 8x8 pan. Bake 350°F for 8 minutes. Cool. Combine first 3 ingredients. Mix well and place over base and refrigerate at least 3 hours. Overnight is best.

Zucchini Brownie

1 cup zucchini frozen grated
1 ½ cup splenda
½ tsp. salt
½ tsp. baking soda
½ cup white flour
Sugar free chocolate Syrup
(optional)

½ cup egg white
½ cup cocoa
½ tsp. baking powder
1 tsp. vanilla extract
1 cup whole wheat flour

Mix zucchini, egg white, splenda, cocoa, salt, baking powder, baking soda and vanilla extract together. Stir in flours. Bake at 350°F for 35 minutes. Poke holes in cake, then drizzle chocolate syrup over while still warm.

Chocolate Chip Zucchini

1 cup grated zuchinni or 1 cup
cooked mashed butternut squash
(thawed and water squeezed out)
¼ cup egg white
1 ¼ cup whole wheat flour
¾ tsp. baking powder
1 ½ cup sugar free chocolate chips

1 cup splenda
¼ cup brown sugar
1 ¼ cup white flour
¾ tsp. baking soda
¾ tsp. salt

You can use regular chocolate chips and it will still be a lower sugar and fat free cookie.

Mix the zucchini, splenda, brown sugar and egg white well. Stir in remaining dry ingredients. Stir in chocolate chips. Drop by small spoonful's onto non-stick or greased cookie sheets. Bake at 350°F for 8-12 minutes.

Squash Double Chocolate Chip Muffin

1 cup mashed butternut squash 3/4 cup fat free vanilla yougart
3/4 cup splenda 1/4 cup cocoa
1/4 cup egg white 1 tsp vanilla
1 tsp salt 1 tsp baking soda
3 TBSP baking powder 1/2 cup oat bran
1/2 cup oat flour 1/2 cup whole wheat pastry flour
1/2 cup chocolate chips 5 tsp 1% milk

Combine first 6 ingredients and mix well, then combine dry ingredients until well mixed stirring in chocolate chips and milk. Place in well-greased muffin pan or use liners. Bake at 350 for 20 minutes.

Oat Toffee Squares

Base

1/2 cup light margarine   1/2 cup oat flour

1/2 cup splenda   1 cup quick oats

1/2 cup crushed almonds

Mix all together until well mixed press into a greased 9x13 pan and bake at 350 for 10-12 minutes.

Filling

2 cups sweetened condensed milk   3 tbsp. light margarine

4 tsp. vanilla extract

In a heavy sauce pan over medium heat cook millk and margarine until it starts to bubble and thicken about 10 minutes remove from heat and stir in vanilla. pour over base and return to oven for about 15 minutes or until golden brown.

Topping

6 tbsp. lard   12 level Tbsp dark cocoa

1 cup splenda

In a heavy sauce pan combine all ingredients until melted and smooth once smooth pour over cooked base and filling and let chocoalate set about 1 hour. Cut into small picies too serve.

SALADS

.a

Quinoa Salad

3 cups cooked quinoa
    (follow package directions)
1 English cucumber chopped
1 small red onion chopped
¼ cup mandarin orange Kraft dressing
½ tsp. dill weed

1 small chopped tomato
½ can pitted black olives
½ package chopped mushrooms
1 medium yellow pepper chopped
½ tsp. salt

½ tsp. pepper
½ fresh garlic clove crushed

Combine and stir. Stores in refrigerator up to 4 days.

Cottage Cheese Salad

2 500 g. fat free cottage cheese
3 mini cucumbers sliced
1 small red onion finely chopped
3 radishes finely chopped
½ yellow pepper chopped
½ tsp. salt
½ tsp. dill weed

½ package cherry tomatoes
2 celery sticks finely chopped
½ package sliced mushrooms
½ orange pepper chopped
½ tsp. season salt
½ tsp. pepper
½ tsp. garlic powder

Combine all ingredients, stir and serve. Stores in refrigerator 3-5 days.

Macaroni Salad

8 cups whole wheat pasta of choice	1 can tuna or shrimp
1 can crab meat	1 orange pepper chopped
1 yellow pepper chopped	1 red onion chopped
5 celery stalks finely chopped	5 large dill pickles chopped very small
1 small bunch radishes chopped very small	½ cup fat free miracle whip
2 tbsp. mustard	3 tbsp. ranch dressing
½ tsp. pepper	½ tsp. salt
½ tsp. seasoning salt	½ tsp. dill weed
	½ tsp. garlic powder

Cook, drain and cool pasta. Once well cooled add all other ingredients. Stir to mix well. Stores in refrigerator for up to 3 days.

Marinated Vegetable Salad

1 package cherry tomatoes	5 mini cucumbers sliced
1 small red onion chopped	1 small orange pepper chopped
1 small yellow pepper chopped	½ cup small cheese chunks (your choice)
¼ cup Kraft Raspberry Vinegar	

Mix all ingredients. Refrigerate at least 1 hour before serving.

Fruit Salad

1 medium orange peeled and pieces cut in half

1 medium apple chopped

1 cup blueberries

1 cup grapes halved

1 cup cantaloupe chopped

1 cup fresh pineapple chunks

2 medium bananas sliced

Combine all chopped ingredients in a large bowl. Stir well, place in refrigerator. Stores for about 3 days. Serve alone or with 3 tbsp. 0% fat Vanilla Yogurt.

MAIN COURSES

Creamy Cheese Mashed Potatoes

5 lb cooked potatoes

1 package fat free cream cheese

1 tbsp. pepper

1 tbsp. seasoning salt

1 cup fat free sour cream

1 tbsp. salt

1 tbsp. dill weed

Add all ingredients in a pot and mash potatoes.

Oven Roasted Sweet Potato

1 large sweet potato

Pepper

¼ cup olive oil

Salt

Seasoning salt

Slice potato into wedges place onto cookie sheet, non-stick works best. Sprinkle with all seasonings, lightly drizzle olive oil all over and toss and place in oven at 350°F for about 40 minutes stirring every 10 minutes. Season to taste great with some garlic powder to.

Oven Zucchini

2 medium sized zucchinis   1 red onion
1 250 g package mushrooms   ¼ cup olive oil
Sea salt   Pepper
Garlic powder/minced garlic   Dill weed

Mix all above in baking dish large enough to spread out. Should be cut into bite size pieces. Season with seasonings to taste. Bake in oven at 350°F for about 30 minutes stirring at least once.

Can also be cooking on barbeque wrapped in tin foil

Cooked Quinoa

¼ cup quinoa   Chicken/Vegetable broth
Salt   Pepper
Dill weed   ½ tsp. minced garlic
½ pkg dried vegetable soup mix

Combine all ingredients in pot per cooking directions on quinoa packaging. Season to taste about 1 tsp. of each.

Chicken Quinoa Spinach Rolls

1 lb. ground chicken

1 small red onion/onion soup mix package

½ cup uncooked quinoa

¼ cup egg white (carton)

Salt

Pepper

Seasoning salt

1 bunch large leaf spinach or any type large leaf green cookable

1 large can diced tomatoes or can substitute

4 large fresh chopped with 1 cup tomato juice

Combine chicken, quinoa, onion, egg white and spices. Once mixed well, form into rolls then wrap with spinach. Place in roaster, then cover with tomatoes. Bake for 2 hours at 350°F.

Can also use cabbage, cook cabbage before using to roll.

Chicken Stir Fry

3 chicken breasts	1 medium orange or yellow pepper
1 250 gr package mushrooms	1 red onion
1 cup snap peas	1/2 cup cauliflower
1 cup broccoli	

Cut chicken into strips and slice all vegetables into the size you would like. In a large wok coat evenly with olive oil heat, then brown chicken use a low to medium heat about 10 minutes, once chicken is browned add all the vegetables and cook for another 10 minutes. Reduce heat to low add sauce and cook until vegetables are tender or to your liking.

Sauce for Stir Fry

1 cup water	1 tsp. ginger
1 tbsp. cornstarch	4 tbsp. splenda
3 tbsp. soya sauce	1 tsp. vinegar
1 tbsp. oyster sauce	

Combine all ingredients in a cup stirring until smooth pour over your vegetables and follow above instructions.

Whole Wheat Chicken Lasagna

1 pound ground chicken   1 can mushrooms stems

1 medium red onion   5 celery stalks

1/2 orange pepper   1/2 yellow pepper

1 small zucchini   1 can crushed tomatoes

1 jar any type you like of spaghetti sauce

1 tsp. garlic powder, salt, pepper, seasoning salt, oregano, and dill weed.

To make meat sauce brown chicken once browned add all the chopped vegetables and all other ingredients and let simmer for at least 2 hours on low. While your sauce is simmering cook and cool your noodles, and combine cottage cheese and spinach together in a bowl. 2-4 cups light grated mozzarella 1 500gr fat free cottage cheese 1 package frozen spinach 1 package whole wheat lasagna noodles to build your lasagna in a 9x13 deep pan spread 1/2 the meat sauce followed by about 1/2 cup grated cheese then a layer of noodles, then spread cottage cheese and spinach, sprinkle about another 1/2 cup cheese another layer of noodles followed by the remainder of meat sauce, top with final layer of noodles, and sprinkle remainder of cheese on top, you could also sprinkle some parmesan cheese to but this will bring up your fat intake. Once all completed cover with foil and bake at 350 for about 35 minutes remove foil and brown the cheese and serve. This recipe should easily serve about 12 people if served with garlic toast and a salad.

Shrimp and Chicken Fettuccini

1/2 package fettuccini noodles	1 package alfredo sauce
15-30 large shrimp	2 chicken breasts
1 250 gr package sliced mushrooms	1 red onion
2 cups snap peas	1 orange or yellow pepper

To begin cook noodles and set aside, also prepare your sauce following pkg directions for amounts, but use skim milk and low fat margarine. in a large skillet brown the chicken until just about cooked about 10-15 minutes, then add shrimp and the chopped vegetables cook until vegetables are tender about 10 minutes. Once you have drained your noodles combine the noodles and sauce to the meat and vegetables stir frequently for about 5-10 minutes to ensure everything is hot when served.

Barbequed Steak

Steak of your choice Rib steak is the best I find
Montreal steak spice garlic powder
Salt and pepper

Over thawed steak sprinkle lightly all spices on each side pushing lightly to rub spices into meat, let sit for about 30 minutes. Heat grill to about 450 once heated place steak on after 3-5 minutes turn steak a half a turn DO NOT TURN OVER after about another 5 minutes flip your steak and repeat has before this will give you a steak that is medium rare to medium. If you like your steak cook accordingly remember don't flip your steak back and forth should only be flipped once has it will lose juices otherwise.

Barbequed Tilapia

4 pieces of tilapia fresh lemon juice
Montreal steak spice garlic powder
Sea salt pepper
Dill weed oregano

sprinkle all spices lightly on to fish push down lightly to imbed spices don't rub on a well-greased hot grill place fish let cook for about 7 minutes flip and cook another 7 minutes fish should be white all the way through. When flipping your fish it best to use a spatula has it does fall apart if handled roughly. Once fish is cooked squeeze a small amount of lemon juice over and serve.

Whole Grain Brown Rice and Pork Chops

4-6 pork chops	2 cups brown rice
4 cups water	1 can mushrooms pieces
1 red onion	1 red pepper
5 celery stalks	1 small zucchini

1-2 cans mushroom soup, this is better if you use homemade mushroom soup In a 9x13 pan pour water, soup and canned mushrooms with the juice into the pan, then add all your chopped vegetables stir to ensure everything is in juice add salt, pepper and dill weed to taste bake for 3 hours at 300

Oven Style Fried Chicken

1 pound chicken pieces

1/2 cup whole wheat flour

2 tbsp. seasoning salt

1 tsp. garlic powder

1 250 gr carton egg white

1 cup quick oats

1 cup whole wheat bread crumbs

1 tsp salt and pepper

1 tsp. onion powder

Mix crumbs, flour, oats and seasoning in a large flat dish. Wash chicken and cut off any excess skin. In a large bowl pour egg white, make sure bowl is big enough to dip chicken in. Dip chicken in egg white coating thoroughly, then place in crumb mixture ensuring you coat chicken well. Place chicken on a broiling pan. When finished place in oven for about 1 hour at 350 turning chicken after about 30 minutes.

Crispy BBQ Chicken

4 chicken breasts

2 cups crushed barbeque chips

1 cup egg white

1/2 cup quick oats

Cut chicken into large strips, pour egg white in a bowl, and place chips and oats in a bag. Dip chicken in egg then place in bag and shake to coat, place on a pan, if chicken does not coat thoroughly, use your hands a press mixture into chicken before placing in oven. Bake at 350 for 1 hour turn after 30 minutes.

Fried Rice or Quinoa

1 cup rice or quinoa

1 yellow pepper

1 red onion

1/2 pkg snap peas

2 tbsp. oyster sauce

1/2 tsp. following spices salt, pepper, dill weed, seasoning salt

1/2 cup frozen mixed vegetables

1 250 gr package mushrooms

3 celery stalks

1/4 cup soya sauce

1/2 tsp. minced garlic

Prepare rice or quinoa according to directions adding the mixed vegetables to cook them. When cooked set aside.

In a large nonstick skillet, spray with cooking spray. Sauté all fresh vegetables lightly about 5 minutes, then add rice, spices and soya sauce and oyster sauce. Fry on medium heat for 10 to 15 minutes until vegetables are tender stirring constantly so does not burn.

Turkey Chili

1 pound ground turkey

3 celery stalks

1 orange or yellow pepper

1 can kidney beans

1 can tomatoes soup

1 1/2 cups tomato juice

3 tbsp. banana pepper ring

1 tsp. salt, pepper, seasoning salt, dill weed, Oregano and dill weed.

1 pkg chicken hot dogs

1 red onion

1 can beans

1 can mushroom pieces

1 can crushed tomatoes

3 tbsp. chili powder

2 tbsp. banana pepper juice

In a large pot or dutch oven brown turkey. Once turkey is browned add all other ingredients to pot. Cook for at least 2 hours on low heat stirring frequently so it does not burn to the bottom of pot. This is great served with whole wheat buns or mashed potatoes.

PEGGY KLEITER

Sweet and Sour Chicken Quinoa

4 chicken breasts

1 orange pepper

1 small zucchini

3 cups chicken broth

2 cups quinoa

1 red onion

1 250 gr pkg mushrooms

In a 9x13 pan combine quinoa and chopped vegetables pour chicken broth over all ensuring all is sitting in juice, if not you may need to add some extra chicken broth. place raw chicken breasts on top of quinoa and vegetables. Make sweet and sour sauce and pour over everything, save some sauce for serving. Cover with foil and bake at 350 for 3 hours on 300. Sweet and sour sauce can be found in the extras.

Turkey Brunch

1 loaf silver hillls steady eddie bread

1 pkg sliced mushrooms

1/2 cup red onion

2 liters egg white

1 tsp. of following spices salt, pepper, seasoning salt, and dill weed

32 slices light mozzarella cheese slices

1/2 cup orange pepper

500 grams sliced turkey breast

2 tbsp. whoreshire sauce

In a greased 9x13 pan place 1 layer of bread to cover the bottom of pan, followed by a layer of turkey breast then cheese. On top of the cheese spread all the vegetables evenly on this layer, followed by another layer of bread, turkey and cheese. Place last layer of bread on top. In a blender combine eggs and all spices when mixed pour over top of last layer, you may need to poke holes in random spots to ensure egg goes all the way to the bottom of pan. This will be very full. Cover with foil and refrigerate overnight at least 8 hours. In morning leaving foil on bake at 350 for 1 hour remove foil and return to oven to brown about 10-15 minutes. This is great for company serves a large crowd without having to make any extras.

Perogie Casserole

5 pounds cooked mashed potatoes   1 1/2 cups grated light cheddar

1/2 cup fat free sour cream   2 red onions

2 500 gr cottage cheese fat free   1 box whole wheat lasagna noodles

1 pot homemade mushroom soup

Cook and mash the potatoes adding the grated cheese and sour cream set aside. Cook lasagna noodles cool and set aside. sauté onions in microwave in 1 TBSP margarine on high for 2 minutes. In a 9x13 greased pan place a layer of noodles followed by half the potato mixture, then another layer of noodles, then spread all the cottage cheese over noodles top with another layer of noodles followed by the remaining mashed potatoes top with layer of noodles. Spread thinly the sautéed onions on the top, then pour the mushroom soup on the top you may not need all the soup. Cover with foil and bake at 350 for 1 hour remove foil and brown lightly about 5 minutes.

EXTRA'S

Sweet and Sour Sauce

2 cups splenda

11/2 cups water

3 tbsp. soya sauce

4 tbsp. cornstarch

1/2 cup brown sugar

2/3 cup vinegar

4 tbsp. ketchup

6 tbsp. water

Mix first 6 ingredients in a pot and bring to a boil. Mix cornstarch and water in a cup until smooth pour into pot and cook until thickened. About 5 minutes serve has a sauce or pour over main dish before placing in oven.

Sweetened Condensed Milk

1/3 cup boiling water

3/4 cup splenda

11/2 cup skim milk powder

4 tbsp. light margarine

Combine above ingredients in a bowl stirring by hand until smooth, refrigerate overnight to set.

Pie Filling

4 cups fresh or frozen fruit any kind   1 cup water
1tbsp. lemon juice   1/2 cup splenda
2 tbsp. light margarine

In a medium size pot combine above ingredients cook over medium heat until fruit is tender.

4 tbsp. cornstarch   6 tbsp. water

Mix water and cornstarch in a cup until smooth, once smooth gradually add to fruit mixture to thicken cook for about 5 minutes. This can be used right away or stored in the fridge for up to 1 week.

Cream Cheese Icing

1 250 gr pkg fat free cream cheese   1 pkg fat free/sugar free vanilla
                                       pudding mix
1 tub sugar free cool whip

Combine all ingredients blend until smooth.

Fruit Dip

* This is great for fruit trays.

1 250 gr tub of 0 fat french vanilla yogurt.

Stir Fry Sauce

1 cup water	1 tbsp. cornstarch
1 tsp. ginger	3 tbsp. soya sauce
4 tbsp. splenda	1 tbsp. oyster sauce
1 tsp. vinegar	

Combine all in a cup and mix until smooth, if you're looking for a sauce this can be used in many different dishes.

Pita crackers

1 pkg whole wheat pitas	garlic
salt	soft margarine

With a soft brush lightly brush pita's with margarine both sides. Sprinkle with garlic salt on both sides. Cut into small triangle pieces. Place on a large cookie sheet and bake on 350 for about 20-30 mins until dry and crunchy. Goes great with cream cheese spread. Which is 2 pkgs fat free cream cheese 1 pkg knorr vegetable soup mix. Mix together until well blended no lumps.

For your muffins cakes and cookies i find it easier if i have my squash or purees prepared ahead of time. When using squash's or zuchinni cook and mash or grate your squash/zuchinni. Freeze in 1 cup serving in freezer bags. Then when you want to use them you just have to defrost them. When pureeing prunes, dates etc I do find I need to add a little extra water.

If you can't find oat flour it's easy to make. Place original oats not quick oats into food processor, and pulse until you have flour.

If your trying to have a dinner party that's low fat and sugar. A great menu is whole wheat chicken lasagna, with homemade bun's, marinated salad, and cheesecake for desert. This will feed a larger crowd. You can still enjoy your party because everything can be made well ahead of time. Knowing your feeding everyone of your guests a very healthy meal that taste great and is filling. Thank you everyone who were my guinea pigs. Without you I would never have been able to complete this book with confidence.

CPSIA information can be obtained at www.ICGtesting.com
Printed in the USA
LVOW061002100713

342103LV00002B/87/P